ISBN 978-1-7321260-8-4
Printed in the United States by IngramSpark

Published by
Fly By Night Press
a subsidiary of
A Gathering of the Tribes, Inc.

Design by Claire Durand-Gasselin
www.clairedurandgasselin.com

Author photo by Wednesday Kim

Fly By Night Press
P.O. Box 20693
Tompkins Square Station
New York, NY 10009
www.tribes.org

© Gabriel Don 2019
Living Without Skin
All rights reserved. No part of this publication may be reproduced or transmitted in any form or by electronic or mechanical, including photography, recording, or any information storage or retrievel system, without permission in writing from the publisher.

Living Without Skin

Don is part lover, part inquisitor, cooing with a quillon dagger. Open your eyes and she'll still be there, standing in the doorway.
- John Reed

Part mermaid, part songstress, part sorceress weaving time and imagery from air and dust, forming acute observations that are uncovered on every page, Gabriel Don's poems juxtapose from anguish to seductive to the thunder longing to shake the foundations of social norms. Her work is a proclamation "from which a lioness—a wild beast stretches." This collection captures past and present in visceral and tactile ways, reconstructing mysteries both in the internal and external worlds. As the poet proclaims, "The universe is as chaotic as me." Don's pursuit of discovery is authentic and triumphant.
- John Casquarelli

Gabriel Don's voice is whimsical and unapologetically feminist. Her poetry fearlessly and guilelessly tells the truth about how the female body is naturally beautiful without the artifices and enslavements of the beauty-industrial complex. Her prose poems are lushly cinematic in detailing her memories of Dubai, Australia and Singapore, and they are among the most memorable poems in this collection.
- Christine Chia

Living Without Skin

by Gabriel Don

Fly By Night Press
a subsidiary of
A Gathering of the Tribes, Inc.

TABLE OF CONTENTS

To Audre Lorde (The Erotic as Power) 1
You didn't want me to come so why did you make me? 2
Untitled Poem 1 3
Untitled Poem 2 4
Untitled Poem 3 4
Untitled Poem 4 5
Chill Like A Lizard 6
A Love Like My Parents 7
Untitled Poem 6 8
Spring Clean 9
candy in my fingertips 10
The Heart 11
Letters to Heartbreak 12
For Dorothy Parker on her 119th Birthday 13
The Boys' Club 14
The Biggest Flop 15
Untitled Poem 7 16
Untitled Poem 8 17
The Alchemist 18
Nobody Wins 19
Fuck The G Train 20
Untitled Poem 9 21
Boroughist 22
J Train 23
I Remember 24
Love: 27
Untitled Poem 10 28
Swimming Lesson 29

Potential	30
Untitled Poem 11	31
Waves	32
You Are My Resting Place	33
We Can Change Our Lives	34
Two Sides	38
Untitled Poem 12	39
Prurient Dancer	40
Cruising	42
Untitled Poem 13	43
the sight of your face just tickles	44
Cri de Coeur	45
Untitled Poem 14	46
Untitled Poem 15	47
Her legs are always open, like 7-Eleven	48
Untitled Poem 16	49
What do I want?	50
Electricity	51
Sonnet	52
A Woman's Place	53
Daily Mirror:	54-77
April 1st 2015	55
April 2nd 2015	55
April 3rd 2015	56
April 4th 2015	56
April 5th 2015	57
April 6th 2015	57
April 11th 2015	58
April 14th 2015	58

April 23rd 2015 58
April 24th 2015 59
April 25th 2015 60
April 28th 2015 60
May 5th 2015 61
May 10th 2015 61
May 12th 2015 62
May 14th 2015 62
May 15th 2015 62
May 19th 2015 63
May 20th 2015 63
May 25th 2015 64
May 26th 2015 64
June 1st 2015 64
June 2nd 2015 65
June 3rd 2015 65
June 5th 2015 66
June 6th 2015 66
June 15th 2015 66
June 16th 2015 66
June 18th 2015 67
June 19th 2015 67
June 22nd 2015 67
June 23rd 2015 68
June 24th 2015 68
June 25th 2015 68
June 27th 2015 69
July 4th 2015 70
July 9th 2015 70

July 11th 2015	71
July 13th 2015	71
July 15th 2015	72
July 16th 2015	72
July 25th 2015	72
July 28th 2015	72
July 31th 2015	73
August 4th 2015	73
August 5th 2015	74
August 14th 2015	74
August 15th 2015	75
August 20th 2015	75
Haiku on August 22nd 2015	76
September 3rd 2015	76
September 4th 2015	76
September 9th 2015	77
September 10th 2015	77
October 18th 2015	77
Untitled Poem 17	78
Untitled Poem 18	79
Untitled Poem 19	80
Things I would look for in a partner:	81
Untitled Poem 20	82
Untitled Poem 21	83
Untitled Poem 22	84
Untitled Poem 23	85
Break Ups	86
Hold the Reins	87
Dubai Nights	88

Lee and Lucy	90
Untitled Poem 24	91
Wedding Day	93
Feminine is Free	94
From Start to Finish	98
Aphorisms	99
oh men	100
Apricots Will Fall from the Sky	101
The Last Human	106
Untitled Poem 25	107
SOPs	108
Untitled Poem 26	110
My Love For You	111
Shadow Play	112
Memory	113
Complicit	114
Untitled Poem 27	115
Focus and Balance	116
The Bar	117
Red Eyes	118
Figs	119
The Buses	120
Cathexis	123
A Minute in The World	124
Woman with The World	125
The Girl Who Dances With Her Own Shadow Still Runs To Love Like The Winter Sun	126

For my mother and father and their mothers

To Audre Lorde (The Erotic as Power)

He was a milksop
   ineffectual boy in big shoes
      and I like big
            big men
   gorillas and I like to feel small
      belief systems don't

  always align with reality
        I am mercurial
subject to change of mood or mind
              fleeting like a fairy
  but you cannot capture me
                my light cannot be kept in a jar
     i am fleeting and free
        an empowered woman
   is dangerous but can one be powerful in need?
   i need someone to take care of me
       and i need to start taking care of me
           i don't mean money
 i mean i want him to tend to dumbesticity
       do my dishes and feed me
    i work so hard
         my mind on many matters
    i forget to eat

         i need him to sustain me
       in the kitchen
  and always make me come.

     know what makes you unhappy and eliminate
     them one by one

      she liked her work it worked her like she worked herself
    with each touch on her clit she was energised and
        powerful.

You didn't want me to come so why did you make me?

It just doesn't work.
I need to think back, way back
A lie that turned into a memory
I repacked my suitcase but the things wouldn't fit

Worked through my problems by myself
They truly care about me too
It's okay when you're really turned on
but then you start to notice
colonisation with blankets
No photos but a sketch on a blood-stained napkin

You didn't want me to come so why did you make me?
I'm hot under these layers.
He was looking at her
The mistakes I have made
The things I have said

The light leaving the crystal is so much richer
but a lover in a double bed,
warming my hands, holding on tight
I asked you for a song and went
off and missed it.

Untitled poem 2

Lover
I gave you my body
But you wanted my soul
And then you fucked it.

Untitled poem 3

It doesn't matter
what you say
about the balloons
Good balloons
Bad balloons
Red balloons
Blue balloons
Lying balloons
True balloons
You are still
talking
about balloons.

Untitled poem 4

A mother pelican feeds her children with her own blood
An octopus has three hearts
A well-thrown boomerang returns
Cannot see the trees for the woods
Cannot see the sand for the beach
Cannot see the notes for the song
Cannot see people for society

Chill Like A Lizard

Why can't you chill like a
lizard sitting near me
on a stone
that skittered around
the path I walked until it realised
we both meant no harm
I sat down on the stairs
and the lizard and I chilled
in the hot sun, looking at
the view while a hummingbird
and butterfly buzzed and
fluttered. The lizard didn't
come at me like your aggressive
words and energy. Why can't
you chill like a lizard?

A Love Like My Parents

The thought crossed my mind
when considering caring for
my widowed mother or father
that it would be too much to bear
so I hoped for a brief second
that they'd go together
not leave the other behind
it would be too painful to exist
if they lost their loved spouse.
This reflection though sad is also
wonderful, that my mum
and my dad found
a love like that.

Untitled Poem 6

You stole so so many many
things from me
but I stole your
heart.
That's the biggest
thing to take.
I didn't mean to though
and here, I am giving it
back—Take it please!
You can keep what you took
from me
just don't come back.

Spring Clean

The apartment like their relationship had begun to fall apart, decrepit in every corner. Being loved is the worst thing that could happen to a person with a heart. Every day when she left their apartment, the roads and pavements she wandered were uneven and every time the city milled them and tried to rework and fix them, the paths she followed became more uneven and sometimes tripped her over. The neighbourhood, once loved, had now decayed and turned dark. Leaving the apartment, she considered leaving him. She looked for the things that had once made her love this neighbourhood, once made her love him. She looked for the corridor of balloons, they had once found walking around together, but couldn't find even traces.

candy in my fingertips

candy in my fingertips
                smile
but i was raised
by a dragon
and
if
you
mess
with my
babies
watch me breathe fire
have one foot on the ground
but i was raised by a witch
watch me
        make
                magic

The Heart

The heart
Cracks
But
Carries
On

There
Are
Better
Things
Than
Sad

Letters to Heartbreak

3.

To witness beauty is to kill it—
We licked happiness out of containers
even though we knew it was empty.

I've licked clean your furniture.
You've turned me into a kitten.

I keep wanting to check my phone
but my phone doesn't have any thing to say to me.

For Dorothy Parker on her 119th Birthday

My young vagina won,
I overheard
and thought, *Oh Honey*
your vagina will age too.

The Boys' Club

The boys' club admitted me
I know I have the body of a weak and feeble woman,
but I have the heart and stomach of a poet,
and a poet of the round table too,
and think anyone should dare to invade the borders of my realm;
rather than any dishonour shall grow by me,
I myself will take up pen,
I myself will be your wit, writer
equal to every one of their virtues in the field.

(Queen Elizabeth's speech to the troops at Tilbury, 1588)

The Biggest Flop

Oh Henry you can't be so clumsy with your cock
I've been waiting at home by the phone all day
Just waiting for you to call
It's a drag
Waiting for you to think of me
Sitting here, chain smoking, raiding the gin cabinet
Mixing myself drink after drink
Thinking what a sham our marriage is
No I shan't be cheery
I don't care if you don't love me when I am sad
I was bored the day I met you
I was bored the day I married you
And I'm still bored
You don't want to have dinner with me anymore?
Because I won't smile
I won't stick a fork in my hand under the table
Holding my tongue
Feigning amusement
At your imbecile friends
And act like I'm not angry
You wasted my day
Locking me up indoors
While you and that fast woman
Valerie, that bouncy big blonde
That giddy happy happy fool
Who isn't married to you
Who doesn't know your mother
Have fun

Untitled Poem 7

You gave her a book
you placed your book in her box
a book you wrote
you gave to another woman

I walked past the bar
I saw you and her
writing—a pen shared between you
wrote a poem together

I saw you reading
reading to her
words in your mouth
sounds in her ears

I found the pages, you edited
her work, you stroked the lines
in her stanzas, giving her ideas
with your pink pen.

Untitled Poem 8

how quickly
the toast now lands
with the butter side up
the door closes
but the lock
is on the outside

The Alchemist

I let my heart lead
When I can't get you out of my head
I think of the time you held
me like you would never break your hold
Memory turns lead to gold

Nobody Wins

You sneer and mock my movement, myself, me
I still hope that in the morning you knock
We are different, miserable one
Misery we made, we brought out anger
All of them looked in worried, they could see
Bad behaviour, neither of us to like

I tried, I tried: me you just didn't like
Anxieties, shakes but when you held me
Everything would be okay you see
High on my happiness down you would knock
Brutal, cruel, unforgivable anger
Why so mean when I was your love, your one

Calm down baby, deep breaths in, three, two, one
Simple terms ashamed use poetry like
Metaphors never used to describe anger
Similes to heighten feelings in me
Victim you say I scream, I'm no hard knock
I pulled you open until I could see

A relationship like ours was a see
Saw of self-esteem

You work with your hands and your hands worked me.

Fuck The G Train

You are not good in
those eyes
so close those eyes
and only sit
where
the
other
eyes
the
ones
that eye you
like you are magic
see

Untitled Poem 9

no one saved your life
you saved your life
you are your life

Boroughist

I can see the rainbow again now the whitewash has lifted. A man in a box hat and dressed in black walks past me, an anti-Semitic dog barks. On the other side a historical facade of a majestic building once used as a savings bank now contains a trendy restaurant or hotel and streets work differently here, moving like avenues do where I come from, north to south not east to west and it irks me like how twelfth street meets fourth street in the west village and when I stop at a local basketball court I do not feel as safe leaving my bag unattended while I shoot hoops like I do in my own neighbourhood.

J Train

Every time the J train passes me on my walk across the bridge, I think you are watching me, my body curves in on itself self-consciously. A person who I imagine is a drug dealer sweats though it is winter and his boom box next to beer cans and litter like plastic liquor bottles line the ground. Graffiti lines the rooftops I am skipping across like The Aristocats and two hands form hearts with index fingers and thumbs. The sun sparkles off the water and a tugboat can be seen long after it's gone, leaving ripples, like the wobble of the ground beneath me as your train passes.

I Remember

I remember being told I left a trail of olive pits, like Hansel and Gretel's crumbs, as a toddler traipsing around the house. My parents would follow the path of pits through hallways and doorways to find me grubby handed.

I remember the first time I felt depressed I was sixteen in Singapore and a glass wall appeared between me and the world.

I remember the first time I floated away. I had to hold onto the street post, tie a knot around the pole, to keep my sanity from ballooning away from the sidewalk.

I remember you, though I try to forget.

I remember lying on a beach towel, over hot tiling, in my parents' backyard in Dubai with a flu-stuffed nose, the smell of sweat, writing adolescent poetry.

I remember feeling safe, my parents invincible and immortal.

I remember your touch.

I remember trying.

I remember unicorns in Amsterdam, goldfish in toilets, minstrels in the kitchen. You didn't let me get my own bike. I learned, like a local, to sidesaddle, riding on the back of your bike, my hands hidden under your shirt, defrosting against the warmth of your stomach. You always kissed me before you left a room. You always said my name.

I remember the day my grandfather died. I came home from school and everyone was quiet. My grandma took me upstairs and ran me a bath.

I remember standing behind bleary-eyed partiers, hungry post night out, among baklavas stacked high, honey-glazed pistachio pastries, dough folded into triangles stuffed with sour spinach, deep fried gulub jamun soaked in syrup, pretzel-shaped bright orange jalebi, mahalabia and halva, ordering Lebanese pizza, at 4 am, with cheese, zaatar, meat, egg, mint, chilli, labna and tomato.

I remember the beach. Water and trees. The smell of eucalyptus and jasmine. Marshes, green, lush swamps and rivers following their winding course, bending and curving, dividing and connecting. Rainbow lorikeets shaking trees at sunset, a vibrational racket. Kookaburras sounding in gum trees: koo koo ka ka ka ka. The song my grandma had for the colours of the rainbow she sang as we walked past a waterfall on the hill.

I remember when Singapore didn't have a McDonald's. The day it opened I ate a Fillet-o-Fish and we moved to Dubai and Dubai didn't have a McDonald's. The tallest building then was the trade center and we could see it from everywhere. We needed a four-wheel drive to get anywhere over sandy mounds, incomplete roads, undeveloped landscape. Clear blue water, a horizon.

I remember you tried to kill me. I spent the day after at the police station waiting for you to be released. I was worried. You couldn't see. You weren't allowed to get dressed when they took you away. You didn't have your contacts in; you didn't have your glasses. You were legally blind.

I remember thinking I'd die without you.

I remember that I didn't.

I remember Kamillas's chicken curry, spooning a taste as it sizzled on the stove. Juggy's swoosh swoosh tea: a weak cup of tea with sweet milk powder. She'd pour the liquid between two cups and as it cooled it became bubbly and frothed swoosh swoosh.

I remember straightening my hair and dying it blonde.

I remember looking up to my older sister.

I remember nothing. I have friends to remind me. Kundera writes in *Identity*, "Remembering our past, carrying it around with us always, may be the necessary requirement for maintaining, as they say, the wholeness of the self. To ensure that the self doesn't shrink, to see that it holds on to its volume, memories have to be watered like potted flowers, and the watering calls for regular contact with the witnesses of the past, that is to say, with friends. They are our mirror; our memory; we ask nothing of them but that they polish the mirror from time to time so we can look at ourselves in it."

I remember I was too young to remember. I remember only because I remember a photograph.

I remember so many songs, so much music in my memory. *How much of my brain space is occupied with lyrics?*

I remember outfits. The dresses I get each year from my mother for my birthday. I remember tradition. Every year my family wake me up, in bed, at 6:30 am. They bring breakfast, chosen by me the night before, cinnamon buns and duck salad or arrabbiata pasta and berries and mascarpone.

Love:
I would give up everything
 my whole
 career
any
thing
for you
but
you
 would
never
ask
me
to.

Untitled Poem 10

You want to protect me
but you on the outside,
me between a wall and you,
makes me feel trapped.

Swimming Lesson

"Don't pay attention to the other swimmers in the pool," they told me. Safe seeming concrete boundaries, water tamed for silly human games we called a race. But I wasn't in a pool and water was not tame and this was not a game and I was not safe. "That's when you lose," they had told me. But I had looked. I had looked into the eyes of every single competitor and realised that this was not a competition. No one needed to lose for another to win and when we lost; when we lost important things like the ground we stand on and the air we breathe; when we lost the things that feed us like the people we love; when we realised the things we fought to win like money and fame destroyed the things we needed; when we lost, when we lost, we all lost.

How do I hold on to this potential?

Untitled Poem 11

I look out the window
and see I am above the clouds
and that the sun is rising
at eye level and I wonder
if this is the time a poet writes
about God
but I turn my head
towards the TV and
watch models competing
to be on top in Bali
instead.

the moon
　is kind to
women
like the waves
　are to
　mermaids

You Are My Resting Place

I like to see myself alone
and out there
but when I am tired
you are my resting place.

We Can Change Our Lives

October 2012, New York City

Cannot there is no place for,
know in all its power
his otherwise curved nature
legendary burst beyond borders
head to head
with you
eyes beneath eyes
like defaced me
ripening stone
fruit.
And that dark centre
Yet that melancholic consumption
his lungs cough, heaving
torso flared
is a sticky matter
still sodden
suffused
with forgetting myself and all my
brilliance
from which a lioness—a wild beast stretches
inside, the dog you woke up next to
like darkness
an unexpected visitor with no
lamp, my software is open source
in this room I relish in feeling
which is feeling
his would not
gaze, his could not
now
turned would not glisten

to majestic me never
low, never missing
gleams and glances
in naive adoration
all of you bask in
its
power.
Otherwise water that remains water
the wine that was always wine
curved continents where hairy
beasts brood
could love, could love
not
dazzle razzle
you
so, it could have been otherwise
nor it could have been otherwise
could wells fill people
a glance is a bucket
smile a fountain
run for the enjoyment of running
through cemented forests
the sound of feet in your direction
placid patters
hips like a pendulum
and not
thighs scratching in haste past thighs
to get distance from A
that before, that was
dark beginning with no safe
centre—a circle is a line
where two points have met perpetual
procreation.
flared

otherwise all is good
this is safe. Safe as
stone. Stone with thoughts
would is, are or going to be
seem so soft it could be
defaced but it has something to tell you
beneath love; love that is a glove that when
the temperature is perfect you don't sweat or frostbite
translucent traces
cascade your fingertips
of a pointed finger, that can't help but be aggressive
the I don't want to hear the words—thought
shoulders—blocks built on my inner vision
and I knew me best but
would recommend the gradual formation of thoughts whilst speaking
not a silent encasement. Words work and
glisten
like fairy dust and cluster bombs, not
a benign beneath
wild wild
beast's grunts, finger furrowing for lice in
fur: you would think of me
wouldn't you? would you
not, I don't comprehend the borders of myself
from the pictures you took of me thinking about you
all the time I don't believe in
the would seem
borders of arbitrary
of skin and nations
itself
burst but not bubbles
like a blanket cozy
a sovereign
star:

for revolutionaries
here and
there, hopefully there
is only peace
no pillaging a
place
that a safety circle
does not surround
not where you and I slept separately
see-saw self and
you.
You, there are many yous and yous
must have many mes
Change your hat and
your head could remain—such is
life.

(written using Rilke's Archaic Torso of Apollo)

Two Sides

Blanco that's been kept in white oak casks
Called
Don
Imported
Domestic
Honey
Patron, patron, Patron

Silver topped dolores
Shredded sweet black
Grilled
Inside out

Lightly
On the side
Served
Super
On the side

Rolled in a
Choice
Deep

(written using a Mexican menu)

Untitled Poem 12

New York is like a lover
a relationship that has settled
into inertia
after a long time spent together
you need to remember
why it is you fell in love
and do all the things
you used to enjoy
doing together
you need to remember
why it's the only place
you could commit to
you need to remember
why you moved here.

Prurient Dancer

"It's all a matter of perspective,"
said Dorothy Friedman
as we danced.
"At Studio 54 next to me was Cher
now it's you," said dancing Dorothy.
Years later, Dorothy asked for a poem
dedicated to Malina and Kushner
who I'd never read or danced with
so I looked and listened
and learned the word prurience.
My demand
is total bliss
for everyone
forever
and I am just as human
as you
if you lived the way I have
I left home at birth
to explore the earth
and when I returned
I was sad
My mother led me to
a tub full of water
as warm as toast
the water felt so good
you can cry mother said
the melancholy life of a woman
when she first learns
she is not a boy
excruciating advantage
excruciating disadvantage
sometimes her body opens

sometimes her body's wrapped in
unavoidable, most often avoidable, pain
when she's suffered enough
and cried, or not cried
when she'd tired she learns
she's old
over too soon or over too late
giggling crazily together
I'm sitting here reading this
again and I still like it.
Lines 11-40 written with words
of Judith Malina and Bill Kushner
I think the line about world peace is mine
(this line was by Dorothy).
I get myself so dizzy.
The process is more important
and the process was fun.

Cruising

different nations
therefore different manifestations
there is nothing natural about CENTRAL park
aren't you automatically
taking on your parents' sorrow
this person we are judging isn't allowed to speak
veer more drastically towards the sunlight
i'm in love with the frantic chaos
this limitless universe

Untitled Poem 13

Is this what it amounts to?
cold walls, cold room, clinical humans, alone
even the biggest stars
walk on stage
at their tribute demented and drooling
and the ones that go through life unnoticed except by the people
who love them
feel unloved.

the sight of your face just tickles
and i try to breathe it all in
              in this instance but this instance
                    passes too like the smell of
garlic or jasmine.

but you will leave
    this isn't permanent like a mountain unquaked
   like my father remaining next to my mother
             unshaken.

Cri de Coeur

Two hands
jump starting my heart
like the two clamps
of car jumper cables
like the two nodes
of a defibrillator
bringing me back to life.

Untitled Poem 14

good morning
good morning to you
the sun is shining
just like you.

Untitled Poem 15

I do not
have
enough hands
to count my blessings

Her legs are always open, like 7-Eleven

Jezebel sat at her window combing her hair with her own hands. She had just finished applying her make-up, her vanity mistaken for insecurity. She decided to do the quiz in the Cosmopolitan magazine she had been flicking through, entitled:

Are you a Whore?

1. *Are you*
  a) Female
  (proceed to Question 2)
  b) Male
  (No need to proceed this quiz does not apply to you)
2. *How many sexual partners have you had?*
  a) Male or female?
  b) Does kissing count?
  c) Don't remember?
  d) None, I'm saving myself for marriage.
3. *Why do you engage in sexual acts?*
  a) I'm drunk
  b) I enjoy sex
  c) For love and attention

Untitled Poem 16

She cried, as I wiped away her tears
as she shook, I concealed my fears
She smiled, as I lay broken
as she clapped, I revealed
my insecurities
She screamed, as I hugged her tight
as she turned red, I turned her blue
She laughed, as
I choked and
spluttered
as she mocked,
I died

What do I want?

16 years old, 2002

I want to dance like no one is watching. I want everything I believe in, regardless of restraints. I want peace, within individuals. I want ignorance abolished. I crave communication, I want the world to articulate. I want to be pursued and envied. I want to be objective. I want to learn and create. I want to be crazy. I want to escape my context and the downfalls of my creation. I want satisfaction. I want to be more involved in the moment, stop dwelling on the past and contemplating the future. I want to stop dreaming constantly. I want excitement filled with stability. I want to feel.

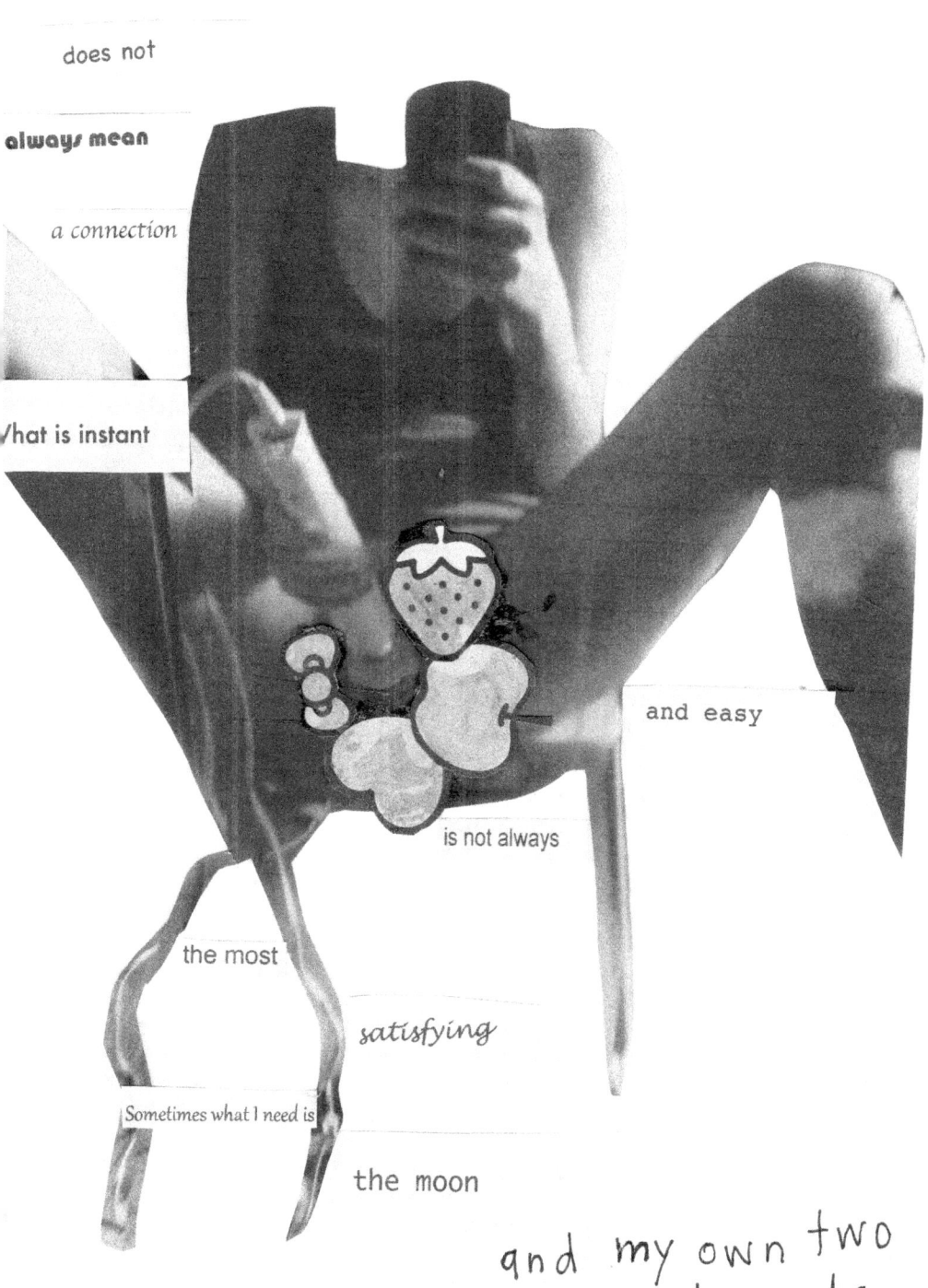

Electricity

does not

always mean

a connection

what is instant

and easy

is not always

the most

satisfying

Sometimes what I need is

the moon

and my own two hands.

Sonnet

Window ledge baby pigeons born, shake.
Their parents nested there, seeking shelter.
Inside a kettle whistled, they awake.
Their feet touched, tight cold floorboards under her
Two birds, oyster shimmer purple and green, took
Turns warming the eggs, guarding them from prey.
Small spaces, heads clash, he strums, she reads book.
Both wanting to go, both wanting to stay.
The eggs hatched, upon the babies, birds sat
One night, no bird came home, they cried alone.
In a bed of shit they lay, decomposing rotting hay.
Mold and fester soured the allies' tone.
Cycle mirrored, bird to boy, things go wrong
Get along, good things shan't always last long.

A Woman's Place

Jane Eyre didn't know she was one, mistress
Madame de Pompadour probably did
Not pair Louis' socks, other woman, whore
Heartless home wrecker, woven tight place
Where women, not spun wives, use sex to steal
Model made masks and casts, for when he goes
Alone she might not be sad like we suppose
Hooker with heart of gold Ingénue feel
Victim girl next-door never base in lace
Vamp tramp femme fatale a cheap threat they roar
Woman eat woman world minority lid
Slattern sluts, mother maiden, deliquesce
Don't you wish your girlfriend was friends with me,
We'd get along, show solidarity.

Daily Mirror:

April 1st 2015

It's my last spring before I am thirty
Tenacity has me over rainbows
Every day I tap away at QWERTY
Around smiling eyes grow the feet of crows
Hard work handed me a basket of stars
But I am tired now flowers harvest
What meaning can you find behind these bars?
Best, breast, guest, pest, rest, zest, attest, depressed
Down hearted, free hearted, warm hearted heart
Ramification humanisation
All you have to do to do well is start
Grow like Lazarus regeneration
The seeds sowed show their fecund head with light
Greet each new day with genuine delight

April 2nd 2015

Hot elixirs of ginger wishing for
lemon. A genie lamp on the desk rubbed
for four. Morning: The last time I was hugged.
Afternoon: the time I shall breathe candour
stretching like a kitten on yoga mat
watch my thoughts roll like waves and grab the reins
in the pose of a lizard, tree or crane
dopamine released as body burns fat
endorphins much needed for the next step
walk in the sun to meetings, interviews
listen to music and consider dues
think of food and pillows after this schlep
Night: Pray for sleep, watch inhales and exhales
and try to calm my inner dark wails.

April 3rd 2015

Sylvia Plath died when she was thirty
Today: Good Friday and Passover starts
My first month of being a wife, flirty.
Resurrection and dying are an Art
like everything else we do them except-
ionally well. Religion comes from the
Northern Hemisphere. Husband Nympholept
says I'm magic by just looking at me.
Down under my family put on blankets.
Daddy I chose not a model of you
to say I do. A revived woman gets
stronger like the North Easter sun. Accrue
her beams as Australia passes away.
Grand time for my final rebirth today.

April 4th 2015

Today's news we knew like second hand smoke
I did not go up on my roof at six,
this morning's astral geopolitics,
I missed the pomegranate moon, red cloaked,
the earth half way between the sun and moon,
angry as a Spanish bull, a great o-
men of change or upcoming event so
did it actually happen, this lunar boon
something that begins with tragedy ends
in triumph, we came between the two round
distant friends, casted our shadow, expound
the sun's energy, we misapprehend
the need to be the center because I
believe with my own eyes, soon I will fly.

April 5th 2015

The last unicorn was sick leading up
to resurrection Sunday. Everyone
worships the moon. She didn't eat all week,
pain and penance, till the naked ladies
magic surprise lilies grew. A new birth
into living hope. Escape from Egypt
is remembered with scrambled matzo (script)
sprinkled with sugar. The days of true mirth
That lovely last unicorn and her steez
Slavery to freedom, light begins bleak.
A weak man is jealous of female sun
Begin with gratitude to have a cup
Though tired still go seek the bright new day
Write poetry, sing, look at art and play.

April 6th 2015

Counting blessings though under my skin itches. Hangovers are a nervous breakdown
the day after needs a survival kit
last night I was acting like a drunk clown
I had a meeting for my first solo
art show. This daily mirror is a bitch.
but this flower shall continue to grow
this swell life shall go off without a hitch
Today I pay for real estate license
meeting with a writer then an artist
put on some pants, a hat and let's commence
Yadda yadda ya—yeah you get the gist
The day after alcohol makes me ill
I try but I want to jump off my sill

April 11th 2015

Move him into the sun—
and sex once
a day has hold of the air and
the world is turning
It is the same jingle of the water
The day is fresh-washed and fair,
we joke: "Now we can die!"

April 14th 2015

"Russia sold Iran nuclear weapons" and I cried
Television is a fearful inarticulate teenager
Rumours spread through an institution
and more than feelings are hurt
but what is more important than
feeling?

April 23rd 2015

I write of sad things
and wonder why I am sad
I research scary things
No wonder I am scared
But a poet must lay witness.

April 24th 2015

G is for General audience
G is for Gangster
G is for Gabriel
G is for me
G Raw
G money
My G
Homie-G
G rated
A G is a thousand
G is gravity
G is ground
G is gram
G is a close friend
G star
G Shock
OG
Original Gabriel
Original gangster
OGD
Baby G
G check
Lil G
G Bitch
G is for gentle

April 25th 2015

The difficulty of choosing
To live one's life
as an artist
is the difficulty of choosing to live
without skin
sensitive to everything
laugh at sight
cry at heard
frown at touch
orgasm at taste
reflect on smell
your heart out on the table
your body vibrating at experience
convulsing at possibility
and trembling at potential.

April 28th 2015

This image is low res
my sister and I
are up a tree we climbed
in France near a river
and my sister pushes me
but I catch myself and
don't fall and break
but resist and she falls
my parents still talk about
the time I pushed my
sister out of a tree.

May 5th 2015

All
   humans
       have
one
     thing
        in
           common
              that
               is
                 a
                   heart.

May 10th 2015

The only thing
you have to
keep up with
is your own breath.

May 12th 2015

At my sensei's apartment
I can see the river and the sun
setting over Jersey
You learn more
from listening.
Marie Ponsot is
to him what he
is to me. She
said in New
York we always
have the clouds.

May 14th 2015

I am the girl between the drummers
No I am a woman in pyjamas
I watched myself in the past
and do not know what I will do
I am that unpredictable.

May 15th 2015

Listening to a lecture
on real estate
can make one doubt
the sanctity of humanity
but that is easily
pacified by a picnic
in the park
with a lover.

May 19th 2015

She removed
the rocks
from her
pocket
and
she was
light.

May 20th 2015

When
you get
what you
want
for long
enough
you
don't want
it any
more.

May 25th 2015

arbitrary lists
a class
of who is
who and who is
not
people with power
make lines
that people hoping
to spot someone
so film everyone
that cuts the line
so they feel less like no one
and everyone
believes the charade.

May 26th 2015

Things don't
stick to me
like
they
used to.

June 1st 2015

I've been a bad bad poet
I've been careless with a delicate art
and it's a sad sad world when a girl breaks
a line just because she can.

June 2nd 2015

Vertical eyes dropping from above.
Angels are sad.
Paisley shaped water.
Serene inducing weather.
Liquid cascades.
They complain about it in Scotland.
H2O descending.
An umbrella barricade.
Clouds condensate, precipitate.
Soporific.
The sky forms puddles on the earth.
I love it.
Raincoats and boots.
I grew up without
in the desert drought
so I yearn for the sound,
sight
and feeling.
An outdoor shower.

June 3rd 2015

Someone take me on a hike
to a waterfall
put me under a tree
and let's watch the
rain drops fall.
Shiver.

June 5th 2015

It is official
I am now a Queen
I can stretch my legs
out in bed, no matter
which way I face.
There is still much
to look forward to
like my Princess days.
My reign had just begun.

June 6th 2015

I never understood giving flowers.
Now I see they are a reminder of magic
for a person in need. Sometimes we need to
see that the world sparkles.

June 15th 2015

Rest is the hardest work of all.

June 16th 2015

Solid rock kept
breaking
and rehealing
innumerable times.

June 18th 2015

It is always going to rain.
It all depends on how you
hold your umbrella
tight knuckled, clenched
or dancing.

June 19th 2015

"It's all a matter of perspective,"
said Dorothy Friedman as we danced.
"At Studio 54 next to me was Cher
now it's you."
The secret is
if you look up
you go up.

June 22nd 2015

you need a mountain
for a waterfall

June 23rd 2015

I am fire
I am waves
I am tree

I am so heavy
but because
the ground
holds me up
I am light.

June 24th 2015

I do not need God as a crutch
I am strong enough
I will G check you
without a posse
I speak the plain truth like a soldier
The universe is as chaotic as me

June 25th 2015

Life is a lot like breathing
Sometimes it's easier
when you
focus on out not in
Exhale not inhale
Giving not taking

June 27th 2015

A.
I forgot myself
I forgot encompassing hugs
Quiet companionship
Running water
hot bowls of soup
smiles in solitude
laughing to an empty room

B.
I can't go anywhere
anymore, "Get out of here
you whore." Oh you
got drunk and
accidentally
touched a heart.

July 4th 2015

It
was
when
I
was
 at
my
strongest
that
I
felt
most
weak.

July 9th 2015

Green blurs
Crunched cars
Factories
Amish getting into car
Rivers
Deers
Horses
Corn fields
Baseball school
Football with father
Cemetery
Urban centers
Riverwalk
Tennis
Oil fields

Christmas tree crops
Cows on a downward slope
A loose moose
Yellow flowers
A sprinkle of purple lavender
Crushed cars
Sun-dried and machine mashed
Rain rusted
Crushed metal

July 11th 2015

There is a miniscule
tightrope
on which we wobble
between
protection
and destruction,
a can of vegetables
a room that smells of ammonia
a bunker for the end of the world.

July 13th 2015

    Jump
  The Universe
Will catch you
  Oh! You will
               bounce!

July 15th 2015

A poltergeist
      [a broken heart, a problem, a haunted past
      a bad future, worries]
only exist
if you
believe
in them.

July 16th 2015

Name the voice
in your head
and tell it
to be quiet.

July 25th 2015

I will greet death
with a breath

July 28th 2015

My mother messaged me:
Last night dad and I were going to sleep
and I said "the world is a truly terrible place"
and he said "you have to think of the good things"
and I said "like what?" He replied "our beautiful children."

July 31th 2015

I got out of bed
for the first time
in weeks today
just for you
and I went to yoga
and the sign read
all bodies rise
and yours cannot.

August 4th 2015

"To think we did all that and not in a shy way."

The mother was late
"denial"
but when she arrived
her and an entourage dressed in black
crowded and cuddled at the coffin
and her mother fiddled with her daughter's
hair and redid her makeup
and repositioned the flower
a few times
before removing it.
Her mother asked me who I was, "Friend? Friend?"
I nodded yes, didn't say, "Lover."

August 5th 2015

Memento Mori

Unless I get out of bed
and write, who else
Unless I fill out the checks
Lick the stamps
Post the rent
Renew the lease
Who else
Unless, Unless, Unless
my heart beats next to yours
in bed then who else?

August 14th 2015

Those days are empty
and I cannot catch up
if I look back
I'll fall over.
Find your Centre Woman.
"I've abused my body
in ways my parents
haven't." Lowell Handler
just called and I promised
I'd attribute
what he said
to him.
My mother taught me
everything
except how
to live

without her.
I don't know
who to
attribute
that to.

August 15th 2015

Don't marry. Once you commit
it is just one more thing
your parents expect you
to succeed at.

August 20th 2015

The word exclusive
comes from exclusion
as zombied-humans become
the system they fought to destroy
after too many wounds in the battlefield
they felt they better be compensated with prestige
two gold stars on each shoulder
but I want you to see me
I want us to hold hands, eye to eye
heart to heart, pulse to pulse,
idea to idea, voice to voice,
love to love
everyone.

Haiku on August 22nd 2015

The silent female
Saliva on bit mouthpiece
Society reins

September 3rd 2015

Never rethink the frilly tutu.

September 4th 2015

I focus on my breath
in and out
and stroke the softness
of my blanket
and I am alone
solely alone
and when I remember
the only one I can rely on
is myself
I will be better
taken care of
when I don't expect
but do
a heart breaks
to create more space
let the light in
let the darkness
help sleep
and when it really hurts
listen to Alanis.

September 9th 2015

The world
looks
different
on a full
stomach.

September 10th 2015

This one's for the heart
if you feel it
you were meant to feel it
you were meant to feel.

October 18th 2015

If you let it go consciously
you let it go unconsciously
what is going to happen
is already happening
I like to hold my own hand
be prepared to be uncomfortable
I let go with clawed hands
practice being in the moment
and in this moment I am
happy.

Untitled Poem 17

We put on our boots and jackets and opened the door. It was cold and wet outside. The bed was warm and happy. You put on my hat and zipped up my jacket and tied my shoelaces. Me too bundled, layered and burgeoning to bend over. I'm now full of holes, memories and blushes. My bag full of receipts, movie ticket stubs, tissue paper, airplane nuts, restaurant cards, boarding passes and immigration forms.

Untitled Poem 18

A force of attraction between two objects is proportioned to their masses but it falls off strongly as distances between them increase. Two galaxies collided and did not merge but changed shape on impact. It is not an ever-fixed mark and is always shaken—love is love which alters when alterations finds. It bends with the remover to remove and should admit impediment. Love is time's fool.

Untitled Poem 19

The road we live on used to have no name, now it has two, though no one would know where to go if you told them, you would have to describe the girls' school across the street, the bank on the corner, the shisha place nearby and how we are parallel to Beach Road—for them to pull up outside our villa on time for our party, dressed in their swimmers, ready to jump into the pool after too many tequila shots.

Things I would look for in a partner:

1. A man or woman I'm attracted to (not necessarily good looking, not a choice, not rational, an unexplainable pull, a tingle, a turn on).
2. A lover. A woman or man who will always make me come again and again and then some more.
3. Openness.
4. Honesty.
5. Someone who doesn't idolize or demonize me.
6. Someone who reads to me.
7. Someone who is passionate and talented.

Untitled Poem 20

Love is a remote, in the hands of another, that controls your barometer of happiness. The temperature moves up and down the thermometer according to their mood, not only your own, anymore. Love is a shove above your stomach, when the pressure releases, when love is over, it leaves a hole. Love is a focus point, from which forward motion becomes possible.

Untitled Poem 21

I believe thoughts become things. I believe that nature has power over me. I thank the ground for not cracking beneath me, waves not rising over me. I believe ethics and morals exist without institutions and threats. People do not need to fear eternal damnation to act out of a place of good.

Untitled Poem 22

Two volcanoes are erupting
The desert is flooding
The apocalypse is coming
And I can't even pray.

Untitled Poem 23

I am an empiricist
I only believe things
I experience myself
I have seen people who think they're free
oppressed by their TV
proliferating untrue images and ideologies
I have smelled musk
I have tasted zaatah
I have heard shukran, afwan, habibi, habibti,
yellah, zain humdullah, mashallah, majnun,
mafi mushkilla, keef halak?
I have felt the sand in the desert
Two Arabic kisses welcoming my Jewish cheeks

Break Ups

a big gorilla of a bearded man broken
the sound of a voice you once loved
saying, "Hi please leave a message"
                              "Hi please leave a message"
           "Hi please leave a message"
"Hi please leave a message"
until the sedative kicks in and
you fall asleep with
superfluous blankets that
smell like
them.

Hold The Reins

a mermaid's chariot
a bath in a busy day
a wavy sea lit
by a full moon

Dubai Nights

Three AM in Dubai we wait in line
Bleary-eyed-drunk, typical Arabian night
All bars pour free drinks for ladies, sexist
We seek pastries, Lebanese pizza peace
Divali, festival of lights outside
Glowing strings shape flowers stars above sand

Highways now where four-wheel drives ambled sand
Nineteen ninety-one we crossed borderline
Palm trees, soft dunes, constant strong sun outside
Little developed to invade dark night
The word Islam Muslim *salaam* means peace
Local friends don't all cover hair sexist

Waiting with breasts, thighs exposed men leer sexist
Hazy horizons *shamal* storm of sand
Some women conceal their bodies for peace
Freedom oppression a subjective line
Gulab jamun soaked in syrup tonight
Inside miens different than outside

We wobble thick humid morning outside
The cute boys we take home shy or sexist
Card games and backyard boozing end of night
Prior kissing on fake island, beach sand
Pakistani taxis past tall skyline
Expatriate friends get along in peace

Serbia and Croatia eat in peace
Sweet halva fills mouth leave nations outside
Border belonging arbitrary line
Penis vagina defined dual sexist
Gender and sexuality is sand
Undulating self dancing with the night

Virginity lost in Middle East night
Wallah matsub it is upon you peace
Time a regulated trickle of sand
When the sun is up I avoid outside
I don't believe in gender am I sexist?
Majnun and moving I can't see the line

My mind is sinking sand night without light
A line of poetry or e brings peace
Sexist people know my outside only

Lee and Lucy

I'm a sociologist
You write I dream

Untitled Poem 24

magpie poem

floating
so loosely in space

though the living
all make the error of drawing too sharp a distinction

sadness is often
the source of a blessed progress

strange to no longer
practice customs

the emptiness first felt
the quivering that now enraptures us, and comforts and helps.

And those who are beautiful,
oh, who holds them back?

Those self-controlled ones know, through that: so much is ours, this is us, to touch our own selves so:

For our own heart exceeds us
See, we don't love like flowers

Girls, this came before you.

Never knowing,
as long as they have their splendour, of any weakness.

Aren't lovers
always arriving at boundaries, each of the other,
who promised distance.

Happy
with Timelessness

you, market fruit of serenity
laid out,

they were still far from capable, still fell away
from each other, like coupling animals, not yet
ready for pairing.

Wedding Day

For Fathima Mohiuddin

"The nicest thing about them was seeing how much they enjoyed each other's company." When we look back we sometimes see spouses (women especially) locked into their nuptial vows, expected to make do with whatever or whoever. How lucky, you have a choice and you chose each other, responding to things that genuinely amuse each other "for there are people who can make us laugh even when they don't intend to, largely because their very presence pleases us, and so it's easy enough to set us off, simply seeing them, and being in their company and hearing them is all it takes, even if they are not saying anything extraordinary or even deliberately spouting nonsense which we nonetheless find funny." A marriage of minds, merged, making mundane moments a magic movie. Touched and tingling. Someone you think is beautiful, thinks you are beautiful too. When Marriage came knocking, lurking and longing, Love opened the door, letting in a suitor that softened solitude. Four feet found themselves grounded in a fleece rug that read Home Sweet Home, a cacophony of I love you, I'm yours. A gallery needs a contract to ensure it can hold onto beauty. The time the two of them talked on the coach, colliding consciousnesses, coming together as two wholes. Salacia and Neptune sometimes swim solo, taking turns and time apart but true love sends a chariot of seahorses who know a shared address. Romance is a ride in the ocean. The captain said be kind, offering a rusted but functioning key to a room with bed sheets that smell like jasmine. Infatuation without expectation, romantic revelation, without hesitation, no reservations, except for dinner and roses. Life, like love, like lust, is waves and marriage makes committed companions who promise not to jump ship. Pirouetting pair prepare.

Feminine is Free

SCREAMS

I am not
your muse
I mused you
I used you
I chewed you up
and spat
you into
this poem

Adam I am not your rib
I was made of me

Martin Luther
argued
we do not need to pay for our sins
salvation is not paid for with money

I argue
being feminine is free
though society makes being a woman expensive
I will not pay the toll

I do not have to buy dresses, blouses, skirts
stockings without holes
garter belts and suffocating corsets

Feminine is free
I am not constrained by
what you think
that might mean

Mary was not a whore, you asshole.
Kali reminds me to kick ass
and my body does not make me weak.
I have faith my uterus is
stronger than balls.

Women are not allowed
to enter a
temple in Bali
when they are menstruating.

Where are the female monks?

Ghandi forced his wife to clean toilets,
when she wed him he was a lawyer
a man cannot force a woman's salvation
her consciousness is hers alone
and what he chooses to sacrifice
is not her cross to bear.

Women flocked to nunneries for an education
when it was rare for women to be taught
anything
when it was rare for a woman to be able
to read
the bible
she believed in
a doctrine she needed an intermediate man
to hear
Martin Luther
translated the bible
from Latin
to the vernacular

If man was made in God's image
what was God like?
Whose image is woman made in?

Descartes said there is a God because we cannot imagine
something more 'perfect'
than ourselves
Who then graces the covers of fashion magazines?
What is celebrity?
What does Photoshop attempt if not
an image
a subjective socially constructed image
of something
more 'perfect'
than the natural state

Feminine is free
I do not need to wax my legs
remove my pubic hair
that appeared in my flush of
fertility

Feminine is free
I will turn back and look
and I will not turn to salt.
I opened Pandora's box
I ate from the Tree of Knowledge
An apple a day keeps the doctor away
Being a virgin is not
better than not
A woman's virginity
is not something she gives away
Sex is something she has when she wants it

Last week a waiter
while serving my mother, father, my husband and me dinner
prefacing his observation
with the hedge he was gay
said he could see my bra
I said I was aware my bra was on display,
sneaking its pink and lacy head up
above my big-cat-patterned dress
He replied, "A man could stalk you out of here."

In a hijab, bikini or naked
hidden under loose clothes or exposed
my body is mine
Feminine is free
I don't need to paint woman on my face
I do not give tithes to nail salons
and hairdressers.
Free is in the eye of the beholder
the eye of a storm
my body is mine
It is not your altar to fashion.

From Start to Finish

April 1st 2013

the distraction of the possibility
is covering
me like a soft bruised peach
I dig into myself
I undo myself
but I've been here before
my body bearing the blows of
my sleepless mind's whims—the
window ajar while
saplings
in changing volatile weather
rear their turtle heads
hesitant—I begin to lie down
but I sit up again.

Aphorisms

You can change your hat but your head will remain.
You don't need to jump to have game.
Rest is the hardest work of all.
When you're dealing with chaos, you need some sort of order.
The creative mind often takes solace in neurosis.
Formulate your thoughts out loud.
The messy mind makes fastidious demands.
Being too comfortable causes depression.
You need a mountain for a waterfall.
One whose every need is satisfied is often dissatisfied.
An empty stomach appreciates the thinnest gruel.
People walk during a blackout.
The fool forgives the fallen following their fight,
the virtuous void of venom ventures to neutral light.
Socialization maketh the man
The wise man seems foolish.
Knowledge gained yesterday is useful today.
Class follows you to every corner.
People would rather talk about the cream going off,
than the coffee grit at the bottom of the cup.
Christians, criminal and convicts can chat candidly,
guilt their favourite topic.
Religion draws out and on the dark side of human nature.
Parents, absent or present, can really screw their child up.
False idols fall fast.
The charismatic can charm for change and coins.
A lack of a belief is a belief.
Not believing in something is believing in something.
Humans are socialized into race and gender
and its privileges and disadvantages.
The dualistic: subject/object woman/man black/white
A person told who they are by the more powerful,
will often believe that's who they are.

oh men

You live in Iowa?
Oh man.
No one's been my friend before.
Now we cling together.
What you saying?
Where are you?
With who?
Let's leave.
Without me.
The troops disbanded
like tic tacs falling out of
the pack
My rhetoric now
like handball
with no other player but me
thoughts against the wall
Egos squashing me
compressing me with
arrogance
Get over yourself
Think about someone else for
one second and you
won't be so
sad.

Apricots Will Fall from the Sky

Honey on cantaloupe, an unintentional pregnancy, a young woman who feels like a bad person, a no-nonsense midwife with butterflies on her white cotton shirt, not a doctor in a hospital with white bleached walls; a husband lying next to his wife in bed, both writing, after garden duty, where they kept a community garden open, watered their plot and other plants; an Iraq veteran who says he won't go back because he won't kill other innocent people, poor people like himself, who are not a threat to him or his nation; a frustrated daughter whose father won't bury the dead bird with her children; the cheer of women talking loudly after too many drinks with lunch, young girls in white tutus dancing around a cross, the boxer who hugs his mother, needing a shoulder, "I just want to talk to my mum," the American privilege to hit people for entertainment, money and sport and fun—a hobby! The Williamsburg Bridge, a woman hiding the fact she is eating meat again from her boyfriend, a daughter grieving her mother's suicide amoung her boxes of poetry writing archival, walking the streets of Manhattan with Derrida, talking to lawyers holding boxes of evidence, the relief of hearing a baby cry, they are alive, they are breathing; people shopping, shopping, boxes delivered to door of things produced in China polluting their air till they can't breathe safely, me asleep safely in my New York apartment with the ground beneath me holding me up and the air letting me breathe without fear and every time we hear a plane we do not feel scared, we are in America.

The climate of the day, thermometer of our society, spirit of the times: anxious. Everybody thinks they got to buy something, buy something and be better. A lot of young adults feel the world is coming to an end: climate change, environmental destruction, politics, nuclear missiles. It is an overwhelming time to exist. Not only do these beliefs and worries exist but these beliefs and worries are telecast on the TV, on the news, on the Internet, on our phone, on our devices. We are bombarded with information, anxious fear filling information. The oceans will rise, the ice caps will melt, the world will overheat. Bombs and drones. Mass consumption of goods that destroy the air we breathe and our self esteem. I need something to be whole. Constant contact, constant communication rather than stillness with the wind. Phone messages, social media and emails, emails, emails. Plastic bags filling the water. Killing cows and chickens, animals for food and overbreeding, overpopulating the planet with the preferred meat for the human palate. Chopped up strawberries, punnets and punnets of unspoiled bright red put in Tupperware to freeze. Vibrating at the limitless universe after watching a movie that awakens what was dead, what was tired, better than a coffee; the book you can settle into like a comfy sofa; the lessons you teach that you can't learn; the people you start losing to the inevitable foibles of life, the enduring love of grandparents. Facebook feed feeds the ego, feeds the wolf that shouldn't be fed, fear darkness and cruelty. Students fall asleep in classroom, a man driving his girlfriend to visit his grandma threatens to crash the car, people push through supermarkets, a lady has an anxiety attack over her laundry, cigars drift up in your window, second-hand smoke, the tree outside the window blows in the wind, leaves leaning back and forth, things that can only be seen in the way they affect their surroundings. The cheapness of a fake wooden bed that cost more than it is worth, the shop that went out of business, the churning white noise of the radiator, the generator, some machine invading ears like mosquitoes. The indifference that is more dangerous than give a fucks, the horrific emptiness, emptiness that doesn't even hurt but concerning in lack of hurt and concern. Hearing "Muslim women and children attacked" anger that blooms into fear of ignorance, fear of the world one inhabits, this is America, this is Imperialism. This is hurting people. Tourists swarm diners on a Saturday, people not sitting here with all the time in the world but in a moment of convenience between here and there, waiters rush, wanting everyone in and out, "More coffee?" Chinatown hot chicken buns, pineapple buns, custard buns, coconut buns for 1 dollar, free music in Washington Square Park, a man practicing martial arts with his headphones in kicking lamp poles, next to hype men drawing a stage with chalk who never appear to actually begin the show, in a constant countdown to action.

New Yorkers who do not have the right to air or view, do not have the right to natural light. Young kids who buy apartments without light, millionaires and people who just came out of Ivy League schools or good schools and who come straight out of college and who have loans up to here so they buy these apartments because it's a very prestigious address, 106 Central Park South, Trump Park, two large marble lobbies with white-gloved doormen. Tapestry inside. Who don't have light in their home because their apartment has a wall next to it, your apartment window is right next to the wall of the next building. You can actually touch the wall of the next building. That wall of the other building prevents any light coming through. Apartments are so dark. Pitch dark. You cannot see anything.

The young wealthy investment banker working for JP Morgan or Goldman Sachs who works eighty to a hundred hours a week, wakes up at 6:15 in the morning when it is still dark, takes a shower and goes to work before the sun rises and comes home late at night and doesn't notice the lack of light and once a month if they have one day off they go to the park and lay down in the grass.

You can throw a stone and hit a poet, a philosopher, an artist, an activist, a person who fears, "If Trump wins, we will all be nuked." So they volunteer and create hoping that their flowers trump destruction. High rise buildings encroach the Lower East Side, people no longer riot in Tompkins Square Park, the end of the tented city, people pay junkies to take pipes from buildings and look the other way, tactics to get people out of their rent-stabilised homes, fire, buildings burning, drugs dealers, the mentally ill moved in making your building a halfway house, a knock on the door that scares your son in the morning, gunshots, businesses unable to hold down a corner, landlord keeps changing, landlord keeps changing tenants, now your next door neighbour pays at least twice what you do and doesn't have a bathtub but he has a washer and dryer and probably attends NYU. The weekends are now noticeable in your building, people in finance and other 'job' jobs go out on Fridays. Buyouts, construction, erroneous billing, incorrect charges. Corporations who send a debt collector after you incorrectly, but you can't send a debt collector after them. The mosaics and street art are taken down, just to be put up again. People protest at Wall Street, occupying the park, still have their money in banks. Gas leaks and gas explodes. Real estate doesn't care. Rome got sacked in 410. All empires come to an end. The wind and the rain and the storm cut off electricity and everyone was kind to each other.

The Last Human

Masses of people hold their devices—phones, iPads, laptops—staring at the screen and whole families in homes around the world are zoned into TV screens, not noticing anything around them, not noticing anything that is happening. Not the oceans rising, not the nuclear fallout. Not the apocalypse. If they aren't staring at the glowing screens they are popping Ambien, Xanax, Klonopin, sedatives, antidepressants and sleeping pills. So numbed by their prescriptions, they do not feel the temperature rising—hot and hotter like an oven—they do not feel the rising water on their skin. Others life hurt so they chose not to feel, too many knocks down and they kept moving but they were dead on the inside, the walking dead. The I have a pulse, a beating heart and I breathe, sometimes walk, dead. Other zombies just keep putting makeup on, buying clothes, consuming consuming consuming, spending money in a conveyer belt chain line at shops. So consumed by consuming, so consumed by their appearance—staring in mirrors—they too do not notice the wars, the world suffering, the fires, the destruction, the evil. People are trying to gather and store something they can't eat or drink, furiously—even hurting each other to get this paper, metal or plastic pieces that when they are under siege by waves and war they cannot eat as sustenance to stay alive. A rich man and his family can't eat the money and objects in their vault and starve to death. Barely anyone has remained human, barely any human is around to the save the world—stay human! If you are staring at a screen to read this, not a book, not a poet professing it to you live at a reading in a Brooklyn Brownstone, if you are reading this on a glowing screen, look away! Quickly!

Untitled Poem 25

People sharing
memes with statistics
the third kind of lie
that banned countries have
never killed an American
on home soil
but a Saudi Arabian, Egyptian,
Turk and an Emirati
have
think about how many
people of that descent will
now be attacked
you breed hate
thinking you love and care
but you are a sheep
with everything you share.

SOPs

Standard Operating Procedures

1. Get sunlight daily, even in the snow.
2. Rebel by taking care of yourself.
3. Have strong female friends.
4. Be gentle, go lightly.
5. Draw boundaries. Practice gratitude, count down blessings, not sheep.
6. Happiness is rain on a tin roof.
7. Rose smelling things.
8. Sleep not too much, not too little.
9. Love your work and work hard.
10. Do not value money, value time. Evil is the pursuit of money at any cost- plastic bottles, nuclear power, war, exploitation.
11. Eat vegetables, make them tasty.
12. Do not watch TV or read the news.
13. Do not use a microwave.
14. Stay in the present, leave your phone at home.
15. Do not consume unnecessarily. You do not need to buy to be beautiful or loved. Do not be consumed by consumerism.
16. If you get your period, do not use tampons, do not use pads. Your body fluids are not dirty or disgusting.
17. Be a vegetarian or moderate meat eater.
18. Don't judge.
19. Be open.
20. Be free.
21. Everyone is welcome.
22. Work is fun, education is fun.
23. Creativity essential, be creative. Write, make art!

24. Do not gossip
or say bad things about people
(don't think them!).
25. Yoga.
26. Walk/Exercise/Sweat
27. Learn about the clitoris
28. Wheatgrass shots, turmeric, garlic, ginger and fresh juice.
29. Witch-hazel, apricot scrub, moisturise, sunscreen and hats
30. Lavender, tea tree, argan and almond oil.
31. Rain and water, oceans and rivers.
32. Build a shed by a stream
with a tin roof
in a place where it rains
sweet sleep.
33. Be in water, swim pool beach bath.
34. Be kind to the environment, humanity, the disenfranchised
be kind to yourself
35. Do not weigh yourself.
Your body is not
for sale
by the pound.
36. Make clothes to fit
your body.
37. Buy recycled clothes,
use your ancestors' belongings.
38. Do not wax or shave your natural body hair,
you are an animal,
you do not have to hide this.

Untitled Poem 26

When the song bird goes quiet
When the song bird doesn't sing
Then we'll find out
That a man made her wear a ring.

My Love For You

My love for you
comes in waves
I think
how did I ever
want you like
my own breath
I don't even want
you as a friend
though nostalgic
I still see you
then a moment
shifts, a shot
then taken, I see your
face—and then
your arms wanted, needed
around me.

Shadow Play

When you lose yourself
              in life
              in love
              in a relationship
           in another person
        in your career
         in your ambition
           in drugs
               in alcohol
            in fame
             in drama
              in society in culture
           in whatever **YOU** lose yourself in
when you catch
    your shadow
        caused by your neighbour's light
           too bright too late
when you find yourself
    in a simple wave of your hand
  catch the black reflection of your
          contour—
     oh what a delight!

Memory

Once you have so many memories, it is hard to hold on to each one like you used to. The narratives you told again and again, do you actually remember the memory, the actual experience or do you remember the narrative, the telling of the tale, some tales retold by your whole family, your friends, until they are a mythology, a fable of you. As time accumulates, there is so much past, how to call on every moment, moments that as there become more, come and go from my present consciousness. Fragments and disjunctive snapshots, blurred out faces, the apartment loses its walls, you don't remember where you were or whom you were with or worse: simply forgotten, gone, lost.

Complicit

People do not realise that their profession, their day to day job, what they do daily to pay their bills contributes to the evils they protest like a bureaucrat naively doing paperwork for the Nazis, the ideological protester today is a cog in the destruction of the environment, the data coder sends spam emails that encourage mass consumption, the artistic director creates images that destroy her body positive ideals, what puts food on their table is the mechanism of the things they do not believe in and say so fiercely again and again while they are complicit in its creation and persistence.

Untitled Poem 27

Who cares?
Who FUCKING cares?

I care.
I FUCKING care.

Focus and Balance

Set your gaze
on a single point
make sure
it's not human
because
humans move.
Looking at a fixed point
a brick, your goal,
a light, a window
even if you are shaking
you are unmessable with
Nothing can deter you
If you focus on a human
those lovable erratic
unreliable animals
you will wobble
and fall
You will get an itch
and the urge to scratch it
You have choice.

People move cautiously
     behind their drinks
   the lip mark is brigh red
  red like blood pulsing
  under my skin under my skin
   heart to hands love organ
     heart to hands hands to heart
   the music plays hips begin
        hips begin to sway
  and the night closes its curtain
      the day can't see
    how red her eyes are
   the nigh forgives tiredness
   the empty room now full
   of people, later left over
     garbage, marked used serviette
          straws, sucked and forgot
   suched and forgotten.

       the day misses the night
    the nigh t misses the day
     they only meet twice

  when the sun sets every one is a p
   poet.
   in the dark all there is is now
   but all they think of is their futu
     future.

Are you originally from
here? The library brought me
here. the dusty secrets
 bound and covered. The boys
the boy's says he has been we
were she was born, that small
town of potaotatoes
he doesnt kno notice her red
tired eyes, he is blinded
by her smile, her energy like
a laser beam, the urge to
uncover her nipples.
if we hide behind words
if we hide behind music
if a smile looks across a room

and stays there.

the lovers left unloved
~~chasing echo~~
~~remaning chaste for someone~~
~~to return to ithaca~~

Figs

I saw my life branching out before me like the green fig tree in Sylvia Plath's story. From the tip of every branch, like a fat purple fig, a wonderful future beckoned and winked. One fig was a happy home and children, and another fig was a famous poet and fiction writer and essayist and novelist, and another fig was a brilliant professor, and another fig was Gee Dee the amazing editor and another fig was Europe and Africa and South America, and another fig was a pack of lovers with queer names and offbeat professions, and beyond and above these figs were many more figs I couldn't quite make out. I plucked and picked the ripe plump figs, a fugue orchestra in my fruit bowl. I ate fast, swallowed some whole. I saw myself sitting in the crotch of this fig tree, full to my heart's content, just because I could make up my mind which of the figs I would choose. I wanted each and every one of them and choosing one didn't mean losing all the rest, and, as I sat there, able to decide, I wanted everything, the ones I couldn't finish I dried and saved for later.

The Buses

The buses, the buses: you are every bus
every bus is watching me. subconscious
my smile goes—was it you? did you
love? No you lusted un-thoughtfully and
never forgave. you didn't remember—
only the wetness of my legs, the frenzy
of my appetite but the smile you
broke—there are many yous many
yous and I feel—what—I am not
ashamed. I feel will another you
ever be mine? Will an underarm
snuggle me safe again—will kind
words comfort. No I haven't been
talking to the bus but one of the
yous is a bus. He is a bus, every
bus on the streets of Manhattan.
When do men turn to public transport?
their gaze on me, their inescapable
gaze on me as I walk the streets
of Manhattan. "Do not let perfect be
the enemy of good" I am sometimes the
enemy of everything, enemy of good
and bad, disgruntled in discomfort
leave me alone bus! leave me alone!
do not look at me. All you buses
trains, present and past, leave me
alone—let me skip and smile and
forget. Let me forget the kisses on hands,
the hugs, the lies, the push
away, the anxiety, the anger, the

I try to please, the I can't please
myself so how could I please you.
no you are not a failure, my
perfectionism is my issue, not
yours but your issues are fear,
anger, jealousy, deception, mental
illness, inability to love. No, you
never loved me. Then bus why do
you follow me? It hurt, it hurts. It
actually hurts more with time as
the possibility of it getting
better, getting fixed, changing seems
less possible or hasn't happened
yet. But Bus do not follow me
I do not want to see imaginary
you drifting around the city.
imaginary yous looking at me.
looking at me, bringing me down
with your gaze, all those gazes
all those gazes watching and
taking and not seeing, not seeing
I am a person, I have a heart, I hurt
I need, I care—like when in school
I was bullied in PE & stoic did
not snap, did not cry when the
teacher came so I was the one in
trouble. I was the victim but I was
strong so I got the blame. the instigator
the hurter weak cries cries cries
and gets sympathy. No this isn't
the bus anymore, this is society
this is the madness of groups, this is

the jealousy one feels when they
see a shooting star, try to catch a butterfly in their nets. No
bus I will forget you bus. you
will become another man, hopefully
a man who gazes at me com-
passionately, a gaze that
instills self love. could I be the
bus, could I be the bus
gazing at myself. how could I
be the bus? the bus is a boy
a bad boy. how can I become
the bus, how can I pass
me on the street, how can I
see me? how can I be every
bus passing me on the street
how would I see me, how would
I frame the picture, the bus, the
boy, their framing, is only my
framing of their framing, how
can I take out all the nails
unhinge the frame, reframe
and look through and see me
the way I see me, without seeing
what I see everyone else sees
how to unsee, how to not see the bus

Cathexis

I mourn for my mother, like Demeter
    created seasons with grief
a daughter makes Hades fill the role
    he will never be as gentle
though just as harsh, a lullaby in a lap,
    relationships have stages, spring will
come again, Autumn mellows fiery summer sun
    when heat gets too much to bear. I watch
the scar on my leg disappear and hope my heart heals too.

I remind myself to listen to my insides,
    which know what's right
        what's safe,
an instinct that when ignored
        bites bitter
    like a scorpion of unlistened to advice.
You will never understand, all I understand of you.
    A husband who died in the underworld,
I know him too.
    The idea becomes a map, I try to
    follow and I try not to follow,
every line of stiches I knit
        I unravel.

When did skin to skin become so
    dangerous? A bed without fresh sheets
and space between us, too many
    blankets but not enough love.
Too many memories better off
        forgotten   but etched on our organs,
the hidden iceberg of all the words
    we use like weapons. A phoenix
must burn before she rises.

A Minute in The World

A minute in the world. The sunrises. The cars turn on. The streets start to sing their song. An old man pauses to look at the sidewalk whilst his dog takes a piss on the path. The fruit is out in its boxes. A man picks between two bananas. A girl comes in for coffee. In a forest machines around the corner turn their key and prepare for destruction. The trees sit serenely without whispering a thing. A slug climbs their branches enjoying the softness of the creases in the wood. The oxygen it permits, omits, emits. The dream of mice and men is still strong. A rat belly full of babies. Night people fall out onto the street free. In certain places they hide.

Woman with The World

I can see my own breath
I feel like the woman
with the weight of the world
on her shoulders
but it is exactly the
other way
'round.

The girl who dances with her own shadow

still runs to love like the winter sun.

Gabriel Don is a multidisciplinary artist who works in a variety of mediums: a filmmaker, artist, photographer, musician and writer. She has been published in numerous online and print venues. She received her MFA in Creative Writing at The New School, where she worked as the Reading Series and Chapbook Competition Coordinator and currently teaches writing at BMCC. Born in Australia, raised in Singapore and Dubai, Don now resides in New York City.

Follow her and find information about future readings and events here: www.facebook.com/gabrieldoninnoparticularorder

ACKNOWLEDGEMENTS

Poems in this collection have previously appeared in: *Apricots will Fall from the Sky* in The Unbearables' *From Somewhere to Nowhere; the End of the American Dream*, *Stay Human* in *Brownstone Poets 2017 Anthology*, *Memory* in *The Seventh Wave*, *Prurient Dancer* in *The White Rabbit*, *Electricity* in *MAINTENANT 9: A Journal of Contemporary Dada Writing and Art* by Three Rooms Press, *To Audre Lorde (The Erotic as Power)* in *LiVE Mag*, *We Can Change Our Lives* in *The Otter*, *J Train* in *Quiet Lunch (Book No. 2)*, *Untitled Poem 1* in *Hallozine*, *The Heart* in *The Legendary*, *Candy in my Fingertips* in *Estrellas En El Fuego*, *Nobody Wins* in *Free Verse*, *Fuck The G Train* in *The Understanding Between Foxes and Light* by Great Weather for Media, *Two Sides* in *Short Fast and Deadly*, *Sonnet* and *A Woman's Place* in *A Place We Know Well*, *I Remember* in *I Remember*, *Feminine is Free* was commissioned by Milk and Night *Pervasive Feminisms* curatorial and originally performed and filmed in the Lutheran Church of The Messiah, *Complicit* in Andree Betancourt film for the *Artists Re_Solve*, *The Bar* and *Red Eyes* were created with the Poetry Brothel Typewriter project where Don is a Poetry Whore performing as her poetry alter ego Dimity Pinkerville, *August 4th 2015* in *Palabras Luminosas*, *Cathexis* in *A Gathering of The Tribes* (online and also in print Unbearables' issue), *Swimming Lesson* in *Pa'lante A La Luz: Charge Into The Light*, *Leccion De Natacion* in *Transtierros (Swimming Lesson* translated into Spanish in Peru*)*, *Schwimmstunde* in *stadtsprachen magazine* (*Swimming Lesson* translated into German in Berlin), *Dubai Nights* in *The Pangolin Review Issue 7* (nominated for Pushcart Prize), *Chill Like a Lizard* in *Before The Dawn* and *April 28th 2015 "This image is low res"* and *The Buses* in *The Brooklyn Rail* (Dec 2018- Jan 2019).

Cento, *April 11th 2015*, was written with lines excerpted from *Futility* by Wilfred Owen, *Contact* by Maureen N. McLane, *spring song* by Lucille Clifton, *Indian River* by Wallace Stevens, *Spring Day* by Amy Lowell and *Sex and Taxes* by Kevin Cantwell. Photo included in *Untitled Poem 1* by Miriam Chisala.

Thank you to all those people who know who they are, too many to mention, I hope you know how much I appreciate and love you.

www.ingramcontent.com/pod-product-compliance
Lightning Source LLC
Chambersburg PA
CBHW071210070526
44584CB00019B/2981